Native Ways

Related Titles from Heyday Books

Grass Games and Moon Races:
California Indian Games and Toys

by Jeannine Gendar

Indian football, stick dice, shinny, and many other games and toys of California's native people come alive through personal accounts, photographs, and ancient stories and myths.

125 pages, paperback (8 x 10), with photos, illustrations, map, index, $12.95

Indian Summer:
Traditional Life among the Choinumne Indians of California's San Joaquin Valley

by Thomas Jefferson Mayfield, introduced by Malcolm Margolin

Mayfield tells the wonderful story of his childhood with the Choinumne Yokuts, who adopted him when he was six years old.

144 pages, paperback (8 x 10), with photos, illustrations, maps, index, $16.00

The Ohlone Way:
Indian Life in the San Francisco-Monterey Bay Area

by Malcolm Margolin

This well-loved classic vividly recreates the lost world of the Indian people who lived in the San Francisco Bay Area such a short time ago.

182 pages, paperback (6 x 9), with illustrations, $12.95

News from Native California

A quarterly magazine written and produced by California Indians and those close to the Indian community, focusing on arts, events, language, traditional skills, and more.

$4.95 per issue, $19.00 for a one-year subscription

For a catalog, call (510) 549-3564.

Native Ways

California Indian
Stories and Memories

Edited by
Malcolm Margolin
and
Yolanda Montijo

Heyday Books • Berkeley, California

Publisher's Cataloging in Publication
(Prepared by Quality Books Inc.)

Native Ways : California Indian stories and memories / edited by
    Malcolm Margolin and Yolanda Montijo.
        p. cm.
        SUMMARY: California Indian culture and history, including the ongoing cultural revival.
        Includes bibliographical references.
        ISBN 0-930588-73-8

        1. Indians of North America–California–Juvenile literature.
    2. Indians of North America–California–History–Juvenile literature.
    I. Margolin, Malcolm. II. Montijo, Yolanda.

E78.C15M37 1995   979.4'00497
                                              QBI95-20307

Editing: Rina Margolin
Interior design and production: Wendy Low
Cover design: Jeannine Gendar
Cover illustration: Harry Fonseca; back cover photo by Tony Heiderer
Printing : Publishers Press, Salt Lake City, Utah

Published by
Heyday Books
P.O. Box 9145
Berkeley, CA 94709
(510) 549-3564

Printed in the United States of America

10 9 8 7 6 5 4 3 2

Acknowledgments

We are immeasurably grateful to Rina Margolin for her careful reading of the text and for her advice and warnings; to Ann and Dwight Dutschke for their valuable comments; to Jeannine Gendar, Wendy Low, Amy Hunter, Robert Zermeño, and Sadie Margolin—the staff at Heyday Books—for their insights, encouragement, friendly nagging, and warm support; to the contributors and friends of *News from Native California* for having taught us so much and with such patience; to those who so graciously allowed us to use their words and photographs in the book; and to the Foundation for Deep Ecology, whose generous grant helped make this book a possibility.

Yolanda Montijo wishes to thank with all her heart her beautiful, crazy family (Mom, Dad & Moe) and her small, jumping sea of friends.

The Editors

Malcolm Margolin is author of several books on California Indians. He is also the publisher of Heyday Books and founder and co-editor of *News from Native California*, a quarterly magazine devoted to California Indian culture and history.

Yolanda Montijo is associate editor of *News from Native California* and Heyday Books.

Contents

Native California

Introduction

Every summer at Point Reyes National Seashore, just north of San Francisco Bay, there is an Indian celebration at a place called "Kule Loklo." Indian people from all over come together to dance, eat, and see family and friends. In the shade of tall trees there is a long table filled with familiar picnic foods: platters of bright summer fruit, green salads, pots of beans, dishes of potato salad, even plates of spaghetti. Also on the table you will find deer meat that has been roasted in a nearby pit oven and a huge bowl of acorn soup.

During the day groups from different tribes dance and sing. The songs are sung in Indian languages, and the dances have been danced for many, many hundreds of years in California.

As the sun sets, people gather around a bonfire to enjoy the

Singers Lanny Pinola, Dennis Burillo, and Bev Marrufo at Kule Loklo, about 1990. They are holding musical instruments called clapper sticks.

9

food and to talk. Among them are Coast Miwok people whose ancestors originally lived in this area. There are also Pomo Indians from the region just to the north, and still other California Indians from the Sierra mountains, from southern California, and from the redwood forests near Oregon. Among the guests are even Indians from farther away—people who may have been born in other states but who are now living in California.

What you see at Kule Loklo, or at almost any other big gathering of Indians in California, is not just one kind of Indian but many. Native California Indians—those whose ancestors were born in California—are different from Indians who came originally from other parts of the country. Southern California Indians are different from northern California Indians. Even Indians from neighboring tribes may be quite different from each other, speaking different languages, telling different stories, having different beliefs and customs.

Part of the reason for these differences undoubtedly has to do with how varied California's landscape is. California is a very big state with many dramatically different environments. It has cool redwood forests where it rains a great deal every year, as well as hot, dry deserts where it almost never rains. It has high, rugged mountains like the Sierra Nevada as well as broad, low valleys like the San Joaquin and Sacramento Valleys. Some Californians live along ocean beaches, others by the banks of large rivers, still others near freshwater lakes or marshes.

The native people who lived in California for many thousands of years learned to adapt to these different environments. If they lived in the redwood forests, for example, they built wooden houses. Those who lived near marshes built homes out of a marsh plant called tule (pronounced *too-lee*). Those who lived in the valleys built roomy underground homes that would be cool in the summer and warm in the winter. Everywhere in California people lived differently, ate differently, even thought differently. There was never just one right way to be Indian. Each group

10

ABOVE: A Hupa house, 1890.
RIGHT: A Yurok sweat-house.
Every Yurok village had one
or more of these sweat-
houses, where the men
would gather to prepare
for hunting or ceremonies,
or sometimes just to talk or
tell stories.

12

OPPOSITE, ABOVE: Drawing of a central Californian underground house and a structure called a "granary" for storing acorns, about 1853.
OPPOSITE, BELOW: A Pomo tule house, 1917.
RIGHT: A Cahuilla tule dwelling, called a "kish."
BELOW: A drawing from about 1858 of a Mojave house along the Colorado River. The men in front are playing a game in which they try to throw a spear through a rolling hoop. The granary on the left probably holds acorns or maybe mesquite beans.

lived a life that was in harmony with their land, a life that was just right for them.

Even within one tribe people are often quite different from each other. One person might be a good singer, another might be an incredible dancer, yet another might weave beautiful baskets. Today some members of a tribe might love the old ways, admire their traditions, even speak their native language. Others, however, might want to leave the old ways behind, get a job in the city, and live in a more modern way. There are many ways to be Indian in California, and this collection of stories and memories—some modern, some from long ago—will introduce you to some of them.

Before outsiders arrived to change things, over one hundred different languages were spoken in California. Even today, almost half of these languages are still alive. Imagine! Nearly fifty different languages in which to sing songs, make up poems, get angry at someone, play games, describe the world! California is lucky to have such a great variety of languages and such a great variety of native people.

Two writers—Malcolm Margolin and Yolanda Montijo—worked together to collect these stories and memories and to write some comments that will help you understand them better. We got some of these writings from friends and people we know; other writings were taken from old reports and books. Although we edited some of these to make them easier to read, we kept as close to the original words as possible so that you could hear the voices of Indian people describing their way of living, their way of understanding the world. We had a lot of fun working together on this book. We felt very fortunate to be able to look at so much wonderful writing, to read such great stories, to put together the words of so many wise and good people. It made us feel very rich. We hope when you finish reading this book you will feel the same way.

1

Growing Up Indian

A Maidu family, early 1900s.

Family

In the old days, the native people of California did not have stores in which to buy food or clothing. They did not have hospitals to go to if they got sick, nor did they have police to call if there was trouble. They did not even have schools. They did not feel they needed such things, because they had strong families.

For Indian people, family was everything. Not just your mother and father, but aunts, uncles, and grandparents fed you, protected you, kept you warm, and taught you how to talk and how to behave. They also taught you how to gather food, make boats, hunt, sing, weave baskets, heal the sick—in short, how to be a person. When you grew up, they might even have a big part in deciding who you would marry!

Here is what a Pomo man once said about family.

What is a man? A man is nothing. Without family he is of less importance than that bug crossing the trail.

A man must be with his family to amount to anything with us. A man with no family would be poorer than a newborn child; he would be poorer than a worm, and people would not consider him worth anything. He would not bring glory with him. He would not bring the support of other relatives either. If a man has a large family and a profession and upbringing by a family that is known to produce good children, then he is somebody, and every family is willing to have him marry a woman of their group.

The family was everything, and no one ever forgot that. Each person was nothing; but as a group joined by blood, the individual knew that he would get the support of all his relatives if anything happened.

Learning

Today Indian children usually go to ordinary schools, where they study reading and writing, history and math. But there are still many things they can learn only from family members.

Today children learn their people's traditions, as they always have, at a very early age.
ABOVE: Carly Tex, a Mono girl, making a basket, 1994.
OPPOSITE, ABOVE: Three Pomo singers, Clarence Carillo, Tony Ramos, and David Smith performing, 1989. Tony Ramos holds an infant son, dressed in feathered dance costume. Perhaps the son will grow up to be a singer and a dancer, too.
OPPOSITE, BELOW: Darlene Franco, a Wukchumne Yokuts woman, using a coloring book she helped create to teach her son, Kowonash, their native language, 1992.

Childhood Games

Like children everywhere in the world, California Indian children played lots of games. They played games because they were fun. But games also taught them much. Through games they learned how to swim and run, how to be fast and strong, how to try hard, how to win or lose gracefully.

Marie Potts, a Maidu woman who once lived in the Sacramento area and who is still remembered fondly by many, recalls some of the games she played as a youngster.

Young people of all ages, both boys and girls, had many contests and races. Swimming was popular, including diving. One contest was to take a rock, mark it by wrapping a string around it, and throw it into the river to see who could retrieve it first. There were also foot races, sometimes in relays. There was competition in broad jump and high jump, and ball games in which we would kick a ball made of wrapped-up skins through goal posts. When the girls played, they were permitted to throw the ball [while the boys could only kick it]. Many times, the girls were the winners.

In one kind of race, rocks were placed in two parallel lines, one line of rocks for each player. Each player had to run to the first rock on his or her line and return it to the goal, then

Mono girls swimming, about 1900.

return with the next rock to the goal, and so on. The game was won by the first player to bring all the rocks to the goal.

Another contest was one in which rocks were thrown, starting with small ones, and working up in size to big ones, until the rocks were too heavy to lift.

Children also had fun with supple [flexible] young trees,

Old-style bark house.

pulling one down and riding it like a horse or swinging on it. Sometimes someone would take hold of the end and switch it from side to side, to see if he or she could buck the rider off.

When I was a small girl, I went on root-digging trips with my mother and helped her collect plenty of roots to dry for winter use. These would be gathered in baskets. Some were cooked whole, or sometimes we pounded them up and cooked them like mush.

I also remember as a child living in a cedar bark house with my grandparents. How wonderful it was lying awake at night sometimes to hear the coyotes bark, and the hoot owls uttering their calls among the trees. Sometimes there would be the running clatter of squirrels on the bark slabs above us; and in spring and summer, just as it grew light before the sun rose, there came the enchantment of the bird chorus, the orchestra of the Great Spirit all around us. That clean pine smell on the morning wind—where can we find it now?

When I Was a Child

Everywhere children played. A Modoc man, Peter Sconchin, who lived in the northeastern corner of California, told about his childhood. Peter was born in 1850; his uncle was a famous chief.

When I was a child the first thing I did in the morning was to go out and play. I played around Tule Lake where the tules and grass grow thick on the north shore. Many of us boys played there together. We used to go out in the high tules, about six of us. There three of us sat down and closed our eyes while the other three went off to hide. After we played this game for a while we went swimming in the lake. We had races to see who could swim farthest under water, or stay longest under water. I played this game often when I was young.

Every boy had bows and arrows that his father had made for him. The bows were made of young juniper branches. We used to go out in the tall grass that grew right in the lake and look for chub fish. When the chubs moved around, the grass waved. Then we knew where to go; we pushed the grass aside and shot at the chubs with our arrows.

The land in which Peter Sconchin grew up had many lakes and swamps, and during the fall the sky filled with geese and ducks on their way south.

Toys

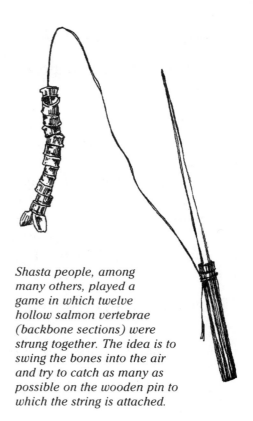

Pomo children poked sticks into acorns to make tops, then challenged each other to see who could spin their tops the longest.

Shasta people, among many others, played a game in which twelve hollow salmon vertebrae (backbone sections) were strung together. The idea is to swing the bones into the air and try to catch as many as possible on the wooden pin to which the string is attached.

With a whirligig, you make a buzzing sound by pulling back and forth on a cord, causing an object strung on it to spin around. One kind of Mono whirligig is made by wrapping a cord around the center of a deer knuckle, so that the cord extends out to both sides, with loops on the ends.

23

Coyote and the Acorns

In addition to playing, children listened to stories. These stories had messages that told children about their culture, their history, and about what was good and bad. That is why in the old days California Indian children did not have to go to school and sit indoors for hours. They learned about their world in other ways.

Many of their stories were about a character name Coyote, a terrible and funny person who lived in the world before ordinary people were created. While in the stories Coyote never seemed to learn anything, children were always learning from Coyote— learning how *not* to behave. Here is a Yurok Coyote story told by a woman named Mrs. Haydom.

Coyote lived with his grandmother. Once he went away on a visit. The people he visited fed him sour acorns. He liked them and asked, "How do you make sour acorns?" So they told him. "You put a little water on them and press them down and about two days later you look at them and they are ready."

But Coyote would not believe them; he kept asking them how sour acorns were *really* made. After a while they got tired of his always asking so they told him something foolish: "We take the acorns down to the river and put them in a canoe. After you load them into a canoe, you tip the canoe over and drown the acorns. Then you walk along the river and you find lots of acorns again."

Coyote believed them and ran to his grandmother to tell her about the sour acorns. The old woman said, "Yes, I know how to make sour acorns. You dampen them a little and press them hard, and wait two days. That is how they get sour." But Coyote said, "No, I know a different way. You take the acorns to the river and put them in a canoe and tip the canoe and drown them." My! That old woman was angry. Coyote took a pile of her acorns down to the river, but the old woman hid some.

Coyote put the acorns into a canoe, tipped the canoe, and drowned his acorns. Then he went along the river, thinking that he would find them. But he never did. He went to his grandmother afterwards and told her about it. The old woman was angry. She wouldn't give him any food and Coyote nearly starved. Whenever he went somewhere the old woman made acorn soup from the acorns she hid away, but she would not feed him any.

Coyote made a fire in the sweat-house. The old woman thought, "He's in the sweat-house, I'm going to cook those acorns." And she cooked the acorns. Coyote smelled them from the sweat-house. He ran out. The old woman heard someone coming as the acorns were boiling. She threw blankets on top of the basket and sat down on it. She was not going to let him eat. Coyote came in.

"What are you cooking, grandma?"

"Nothing."

"I smell acorns." He stood around. "I hear something boiling."

"No," said the old woman.

"No," he said, "I hear something boiling."

Then Coyote seized her and lifted her up. He found the acorns. He ate them, for he was almost starved.

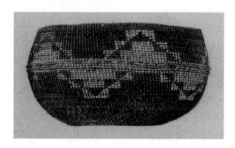

A basketry bowl. The Yurok and their neighbors ate acorn soup out of these beautiful baskets.

Learning to Hunt

Boys and girls played together when they were little, but as they grew older they often learned to do different things. Girls would spend much more of their time with their mothers and their aunts. They would help them collect materials for their baskets and gather plants for food and medicine. By helping, the girls would eventually learn what they needed to know about becoming adult members of a family and community.

Boys, meanwhile, would begin to follow their fathers, uncles, and other men, learning how to hunt, fish, and behave properly. When a boy went hunting, he would not necessarily eat the meat of the animal he caught. He would give it to his family, and maybe even eat none of it. The family would give him food that his brothers or cousins had gotten. That way, he learned to support his family and he also learned that they could support him. Jim McCarthy, a Kumeyaay man from southern California, recalled how he learned to hunt.

When I was a boy I always hunted with my father's younger brother. I remember when he first took me hunting. I had a small bow and arrows. My uncle told me to poke into a packrat's nest with a long stick. I asked him instead to let me shoot when the packrat sat outside, but he said, "No, you can't wound him." I insisted and shot, but the arrow failed to penetrate for lack of power. I cried and shuffled my feet. My uncle told me that it was no use for me to try, anyway, because he would not let me eat it.

Up to the time I married I never ate what I killed. Others can eat the game, but a boy cannot eat his kill until he is adult. One who refrains is always lucky. When I was a grown boy, whenever I went to hunt, I killed several rabbits almost immediately.

Snares, Nets, and Traps

Although we usually think of Indian people hunting with bows and arrows, they had many interesting ways of catching animals.

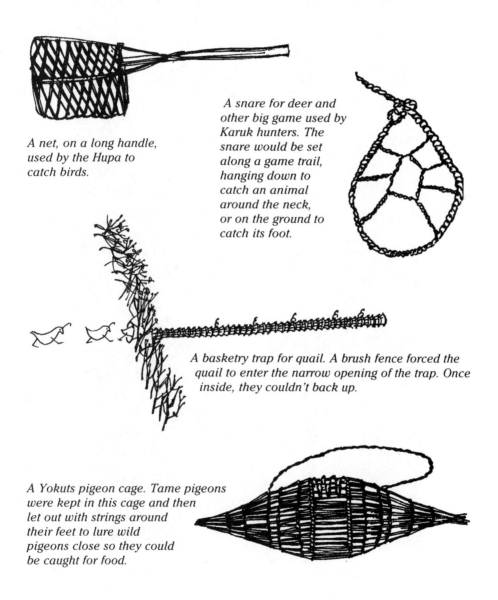

A net, on a long handle, used by the Hupa to catch birds.

A snare for deer and other big game used by Karuk hunters. The snare would be set along a game trail, hanging down to catch an animal around the neck, or on the ground to catch its foot.

A basketry trap for quail. A brush fence forced the quail to enter the narrow opening of the trap. Once inside, they couldn't back up.

A Yokuts pigeon cage. Tame pigeons were kept in this cage and then let out with strings around their feet to lure wild pigeons close so they could be caught for food.

A dancer at Kule Loklo, 1993.

A Girl's Dance Song

When a girl became a woman or a boy became a man, there was sometimes a special celebration. For a girl this often meant being alone for several days in a specially made little house, except when visited by mother and aunt, who would tell her all kinds of things about what it was like to be an adult. Then sometimes a big dance would be held. After that she was expected to be more responsible, and soon people would be thinking about whom she would marry.

Here is a translation of a song the Wintu people used to sing to a girl who had become a woman. It was recorded around 1870.

Thou art a girl no more,
Thou art a girl no more;
The chief, the chief,
The chief, the chief,
Honors thee
In the dance, in the dance,
In the long and double line
Of the dance,
Dance, dance,
Dance, dance.

Becoming a Man

People also marked the time when a boy became a man. Among some groups, the boy would undergo special training. The elders would teach him men's songs and dances and special prayers. He might be expected to do something brave as well, to spend a night alone in the woods or dive into a lake to receive the dreams and powers he would need to be successful.

Samson Grant, an Atsugewi man well known for his abilities to cure the sick, talked about how he became a man.

I wanted to know about history, so I used to go to the old people every evening. I fixed my bed where an old man was. This old man knew about how the world was made. He knew how people once lived. He knew how to live and what to do. He told me: "First thing in the morning you get up and you go out to the spring. You take a bath every morning."

So I took a bath every morning, and I kept on running every night until my voice changed.

My father was watching for this. My father said to me, "Now, my son, you listen to me. Your voice changed, and I want you to go to the mountain to the big lake. You take five loads of wood to the mountain. On the top of the mountain build a fire so that I can see it. Then go to the lake. Make a big jump into the lake and dive right down. When you get to the bottom, take a mouthful of water; wash your mouth out. Spit this water out and take another mouthful and swallow it before you come to the top of the water."

Then he said, "You make a big fire on the top of the mountain. You do this five times tonight and I will watch you. After you fix the fires, fix your bed. Just sit up and don't sleep. Get some rocks and pile them up. Pick up a rock and throw it toward the east; then pick up another rock and throw it toward the west; then pick up another rock and throw it toward the west; then pick up another rock and throw it toward the south.

"When you have done this, take another rock and make a pillow out of it. Then you will dream something. Maybe you will dream of winning at gambling or of a hunter killing a deer or about doctoring. If you dream one of these things, you must remember it. Don't go back in the water again; don't throw those dreams away. Come right back. When you come to the house, come to that tree. I'll watch for you.

"If you don't come back, I'll know that you didn't dream of those things, so then I will think you dreamed something bad. If you dreamed something bad, you must go into the water and swim again and throw the bad dreams away."

That is what he told me.

When I came back, I was a man, no longer a boy.

An Atsugewi sweat-house. The men often slept in houses such as this, and younger boys who wanted to learn would often be invited to sleep here as well. The inset photo shows Samson Grant as an old man, in 1922.

Getting Married

Family ties were so great that when it came time to choose a wife or husband, the family might have a pretty big part in the decision. Let's say that a boy and a girl began to like each other and want to get married. The boy might first talk with the girl, but he would also ask his parents' permission. And his parents or some other family member would then go to the girl's family and talk it over with them. In many places a marriage proposal meant that the boy's family would have to give many valuable gifts to the girl's family as a wedding gift. The families would then decide whether or not the marriage was a good one, because it wasn't just a boy and a girl getting married. Remember, families were very strong and it was a member of one family marrying a member of the other. What if the girl or boy was lazy? Such a person would become a burden to the family they married into.

In 1936, Jeff Jones, a Nomlaki man about 70 years old, told how marriages used to be arranged among his people.

When a young man is about twenty, his family will want to make a match for him; so they talk to the parents of some girl. The boy will take the hint and drop the game he has hunted in front of her door. He will always leave over half of what he gets. He will also haul wood for her parents.

Then, when the girl gets old enough to be married, the old folks try to make the match. The boy's parents carry over some property, and the girl keeps these things if she wants him. If she refuses him, the boy's family demands pay for all the work he has done. The boy won't make the demand himself, but his parents will insist on repayments for what he has done for her. Her parents might talk her into the marriage, and she might give in, even if she doesn't care so much for him. They say that people married in this way get along better than when they love each other.

When the girl is old enough to get married, the aunt brings in the news to the man's family and after a while this aunt takes the news back to the girl. A woman has to do this. Then an aunt or first cousin living in the same house with the man is usually sent to take beads [money] to the girl's parents. If she accepts, then she can expect a husband.

A Nisenan bride. The shell beads she is wearing are money, showing that she is a wealthy person, the wife of a chief. Photo taken around 1870.

Tarantula

After people got married, did they live happily ever after? Sometimes they did, sometimes they didn't. In this funny story told by the Coast Yuki people, the wife discovers that her husband, named Tarantula, is amazingly stupid. He does everything all wrong!

There was a man named Tarantula. He had a wife. Tarantula did not know much. His wife had to tell him everything.

They built a dwelling house. They got redwood bark for the sides. They kept at it until it was finished. She told him: "When you finish the house put earth around the bottom." He went out and threw up earth. He kept throwing up earth, until the house was all buried. She went out to see what he was doing. There he was throwing up earth as fast as he could.

"You crazy thing, what is the matter with you?" she asked. "You ought to go off; you don't know anything." They finished the house. Everything was done.

One day it was raining. The house was leaking. She said, "You'd better go out and find some redwood bark to stop this leak." He went on top of the house and lay his body over the leaky place, instead of getting bark. He lay there a long time and his wife did not know what had become of him. He almost died of the cold, as he lay there wet and shivering.

"I'd like to know what's the matter with you," she said. "You don't know anything, you crazy thing."

2

Many Kinds of People

A Pomo village, 1880s.

Many Kinds of People

There were many different ways of living in old California. In some places native people lived in wooden houses, in some places they lived in thatched houses, in some places they lived in earth-covered houses dug well into the ground. Where food was plentiful—such as along the coast near what is now Santa Barbara—people lived in large towns of a thousand or more. Where food and water were scarce, such as in the desert, people lived in small bands, usually just families, and moved constantly over large areas to hunt the game or gather the crops they needed to live.

Generally, though, people lived in villages. These villages were usually fairly small, maybe ten or so homes. If you grew up in one of these villages, you would know everyone, and everyone would know you. You would also know everyone in the nearby villages. Months might pass without your ever seeing a stranger.

In these small villages, there were many kinds of people. Some people were strong, some not so strong; some were kind, others grouchy; some people were generous, others greedy; some people were happy, while others complained about everything; some people were obedient and followed the rules, while others were always getting into trouble.

Almost all men hunted and fished and almost all women gathered plant foods and made baskets. Yet people also had special talents and special skills. One person might be a skilled warrior, for example. Someone else might be a trader, a healer, or (if he could run fast and had a good memory) a messenger who could carry information from one village to another. If a person was especially well thought of, could speak well and influence others, and was looked up to as a leader, this person might be considered the headman, or chief.

Here is how a Hupa man once described such a leader. Captain John, as he was called, lived around 1900.

Captain John

Captain John was a good man. He was sort of a religious fellow, and he always talked to the people. Old John told them how to act, what to say, and things like that. He was good to everyone. The other people depended on John some. He always was good to them. He knew the laws, and he told others about them. He was always telling young folks what was right and what was wrong. Anything he had, he divided up with others. Sometimes he would get a whole boatload of eels or salmon and give them all away. He gave them to the old people, everyone. Old John would give away the last thing he had. He was a good man, but if you got into trouble with him, look out! He didn't stand back for no one.

Choosing a Chief

In the old days, the chief was generally a man, but sometimes a woman might be chosen. While chiefs had a lot of importance, they were not like bosses or dictators. They did not give orders and expect people to obey them. Indeed, if a chief lost the confidence of his people, he might try to tell them what to do, but the people would simply ignore him and walk away. Chiefs were leaders because they were respected. Rather than ruling by strength, they ruled by what is called "consensus"—getting everyone to agree.

Chiefs had many responsibilities. If it was a difficult time—if there was fighting with neighbors or if food was scarce or if people were quarreling or misbehaving—the people of the village would look toward the chief to help them out.

Patrick Miguel, a Quechan man, once described how a chief was chosen.

You know how some men are quick and strong and know the things to do, how people like to do things for them, and how they have a gift for getting everybody cheerful? Well, those men are leaders. When a man knew he had the power to be a good leader, he told his dreams. If his dreams were good, his plans would be followed, but if they were poor, others would tell him so and he could do nothing. Sometimes men struggled with each other to lead war parties and arrange daily affairs. Then each would try to get more of the people on his side, giving feasts to his friends and encouraging them to speak of his wisdom. But it was not long before we knew who was the better man and he became leader. If a leader acted badly, it meant his power had deserted him and it was time to have another to decide things.

Today's Leaders

In modern times, Indian communities have had to develop different kinds of leaders. These may be the chairwoman or chairman of a tribe, or maybe the president of an organization. Such a person is chosen by election. Yet even today, leaders generally have to seek consensus from the people, and they must continually show that they are worthy of respect. Even today individual families still hold a lot of power. After all, the old ways worked for thousands of years. Why change now?

Two contemporary leaders in Indian communities. Katherine Saubel (Cahuilla, in the photo on the left from 1992) is chairwoman of the board of the Morongo Reservation's Malki Museum (near Banning), and a member of the California Native American Commission. David Risling, Jr. (Hupa/Karuk/Yurok) is co-founder of a Native American university (D-Q University) and helped found many organizations, including California Indian Legal Services, the California Indian Education Association, and the Native American Rights Fund.

Training to be a Warrior

Everywhere in the world, people have warfare. So did California Indians. But their wars were different from those of our time because they were often on a much smaller scale, so that as few people as possible were killed. They did not like wars very much, and more importantly, they understood how to end them.

Perhaps one reason that wars were small is that each group of people lived in a territory that they knew well, and one that was able to support them. Communities also had fairly small populations, so they did not have the kinds of wars that people have when they need more room. In fact, when they fought it was rarely to conquer another group and take over their land. It was usually because they were angry and felt that another person or his or her tribe had insulted them in some way. After a brief fight, maybe someone would get wounded or even one or two people would get killed. But that would be enough to satisfy the anger, and the war would stop. Then the winners would settle the war by giving gifts for the people they had killed, and in this way the war would end. Because the winners had to give gifts, they were usually careful not to kill many people.

California Indians, like people everywhere, did not live in perfect peace. Still, they were wise in their ways of keeping wars small, and we have a lot to learn from studying how they did this.

Jeff Jones, a Nomlaki man, once recalled how a man got to be a good warrior.

A warrior is trained by being shot at with blunt arrows. He has to learn to dodge them. They practice that way. This dodging is call *t'eya*. Those who can't dodge are advised to stay out of the thick of battle. Such a man might go to war, but he would stay in the back because they put the best in front. Good dodgers do this almost without moving. Some shots come quick and are hard to dodge, so it is necessary to turn one's side to the enemy. The wobbling shots are harder to dodge than the straight ones.

They have good runners and fighters picked out for war. Those who can't run or shoot well can't get into war. They pick the men like they do a ball team. It takes a good runner to run with the armor. Warriors don't get anything for fighting. They have to practice to be good fighters. They hunt and have foot races, wrestle, carry wood, and practice lifting for warfare.

Pomo warrior in armor to protect his body.

Messengers

There were over five hundred tribal groups in California—
like little nations, really—most of them numbering no more than
a few hundred people. Each group lived in its own valley and
its members often felt that they alone were the "real" people.
Everyone else, they would say, had strange habits, spoke funny
languages, and did things all wrong.

Yet, despite this, each of these small tribal groups needed its
neighbors for trading, for marriage partners, or simply for enter-
tainment. Life in these small worlds could get a little boring.
After a long winter, when everyone had been kept home too
long by rains and muddy trails, the urge to have a party was
especially strong. The chief would call upon his messengers.
Messengers were men especially trained as runners, who had
good memories so they could repeat complicated instructions.
The messengers would be sent to other villages.

Jeff Jones, a Nomlaki man, recalls how it was.

Our people dance every spring and have all kinds of dances.
When everything is all very green, when winter is over and
everything is warm and the sun is coming north, when the
birds holler *witwitwit*, the people begin to ask, "Why can't we
play a little?" Then they send news to their close neighbors
that they are going to have a dance.

The messenger who announces the dance-feast to neighboring villages and invites people has strings with knots in
them—one for each day until the dance is to start. One string
is given to each headman of a village, and every day the
headman unties one knot until they are all untied. The first
knot is untied on the day that the messenger delivers it. The
people come on the day the last knot is untied. The Indians
used to laugh about this custom because now they can just
say, "Next Saturday."

Trading

People everywhere loved to trade. Perhaps a people who lived along the coast had plenty of abalone shells with which to make jewelry. But they did not have good, strong wood for making bows. They could trade with the people who lived inland, giving them some of their abalone shells and getting wood for bows. In this way, trading allowed everyone to come out ahead.

Trading was also fun and adventurous. It meant you could meet other people, even people who spoke a different language. If meant you could touch new materials, see new things, even eat new foods. When you returned to your village you would have new stories to tell, maybe a new game to play, interesting news from other places.

Here is how Jeff Jones, a Nomlaki man, remembered the traders of his village:

Once there were two fellows who roamed around from place to place to trade. The folks kind of got after them. "Why do you go around to trade; why don't you let them come here?" they would ask. "If I stay home," they answered, "I won't learn anything. By going from place to place I learn more, I learn other people's ways and how they act and treat each other. If I stay here, I don't see anything and can't learn anything. By traveling around I learn more of different things, of talking. By going around I trade for things that I don't want, but I take them to the next place and trade for something else. When I trade for something that I care for or that would be handy to me, I keep it."

California Indians had money, but instead of using silver or other metals they used rare or carefully worked shells.
ABOVE: A Tolowa man measures a string of long dentalia shells against marks tattooed on his arm.
BELOW: Many people used clam shell disks strung together as money.

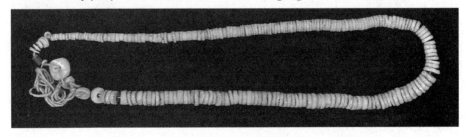

Essie Parrish was a famous healer and a leader of the Kashaya Pomo people. Here she is wearing a special dress and carrying special staves that give her spiritual power.

Doctoring

In the old days, California Indians did not have many of the diseases and sicknesses that people in other parts of the world had, or that people have today. Most especially, they did not have contagious diseases like smallpox, measles, mumps, or AIDS. Still, of course, people got sick. For some sicknesses, a doctor was summoned. Such a doctor is sometimes called a shaman or maybe a medicine woman or medicine man.

Doctors were sometimes family members, sometimes simply people one knew who had special powers. The family of the sick person paid the doctor to come, and the doctor would look the person over to see if the illness could be found. Often the doctor would pray or sing songs or even dance to increase power and summon spiritual help. It was often felt that the illness was a thing, something real and evil, that had entered the patient, and when the doctor found where it was, then the illness would be sucked out and removed.

Most Indian people today go to regular doctors and dentists, and most of them buy their medicines in drugstores. There are, though, still some old-time doctors who do curing, and sometimes Indian people still see such doctors. Many feel that Indian doctors are sometimes able to cure diseases that ordinary doctors can't cure.

One of the most famous native doctors in California was a Pomo woman named Essie Parrish. Although she died in 1979, she is still widely remembered by her family and by many others for all the wonderful work she did, for all the people she helped. Speaking her own language, Kashaya Pomo, Mrs. Parrish told how she first cured someone. It was translated into English by a linguist (language expert) named Robert Oswalt.

I am going to tell about treating people, since you want to know these things about me. I have been a doctor and will be one for all my life on this earth. I was put here on earth to cure people.

The first person I cured was when I was a little more than twelve years old. At that time white doctors were hard to find; we were far away from any medicine doctor.

One time my younger sister fell sick. She was so extremely sick that they thought she would die. Unexpectedly they summoned me from inside the house. I still remember that; that was towards four o'clock in the evening.

When he had called me into the house my great-uncle said, "Couldn't you do something for your little sister?"

I wonder what I should do now, I was thinking to myself because I was little and didn't know. But I said, "All right" because my power had told me, "If anyone ever asks anything of you, you should not say no. You are not for that purpose. You are one who fixes people. You are one who cures people." That's why I said, "All right."

After I had agreed, I prayed to heaven. My right hand I put on her head. When I had done so, a song that I didn't know came down into me. Amazingly that song came up out of me. But I didn't sing it out loud; it was singing down inside of me. "I wonder how I am going to cure her," I was thinking to myself. To my amazement she got well a few days afterward. That was the first person I cured.

The Beautiful Trail

When a California Indian died, the body was usually burned or buried. Sometimes beautiful things like necklaces and powerful stones would be buried with the person. Also, the person's possessions would often be destroyed. A woman's baskets and clothes, for example, might be thrown into the fire or buried with her body. People did not want to have those things around.

In the old days in some tribes, when someone died people burned all of his or her possessions— clothes, tools, even the most beautiful and valuable of baskets. This picture of preparations for such a "burning" at a Maidu funeral was taken in 1908.

It would make them too sad, and it was felt that these objects would miss the person who had died. And the person would miss the objects, and the ghost might come back. It was best to get rid of the objects and send the dead off to the next world.

It was not polite to speak the name of a person who had died. If someone mentioned the name of a dead relative, you would get very angry. It would be like swearing is among us today— it would be very insulting. Maybe this is how people protected themselves against the great pain of missing someone who had died.

Many Indian people believed that the spirit of the person who died went to another world. Often this other world was much like this one, except that things were done backwards. Night was day and day was night, for example. Some people thought that this other world was fairly happy, and people danced all the time. Others thought it was sad.

According to the Wintu people, the spirit of the dead climbed Mount Shasta and then walked along the Milky Way to the land of the dead. The Milky Way was called the "spirit trail" or the "flower trail." Here is a speech given to the dead, urging them to leave this world.

You are dead.
You will go above there to the trail.
That is the spirit trail.
Go there to the beautiful trail.
May it please you not to walk about where I am.
You are dead.
Go there to the beautiful trail above.
That is your way.
Look at the place where you used to wander.
The north trail, the mountains where you used to wander,
   you are leaving.
Listen to me: go there!

3

A Land of Plenty

A Wintu couple, Rosa Charles and Billy George, digging for roots, 1931.

A Rich Harvest

Potatoes, carrots, onions, yams—people today eat many roots, and so did California Indians in the old days. A favorite was the bulb of a flower which we call brodiaea, or sometimes "Indian potato." This tall, elegant blue flower had a little bulb, and when the time was right the women would go out into their fields and collect lots and lots of them, filling up big baskets with these delicious little bulbs. To dig them out of the ground, they used a "digging stick," a tool made of a very hard wood with a sharp point. This sharp stick could be poked into the earth underneath the root, and then the root could be pried up easily.

Indian women collected brodiaea bulbs for thousands of years, yet their meadows never ran out. Each year, in fact, when the women returned to their meadows, there seemed to be even more bulbs than there had been the year before. How could this be? Part of the secret has to do with the way in which the women collected the bulbs. They would collect bulbs only at a special time of year, when they knew that the bulbs were at their ripest and when tiny bulblets were beginning to form around them. They would loosen the soil with their digging sticks, pluck out a bulb, and rub off the dirt. With the dirt they would rub off the tiny bulblets, scattering them over the loosened soil. When the fall rains came, these bulblets would sprout and grow. Thus, the more bulbs people gathered, the more of these beautiful and delicious plants would grow the next year. By doing things the right way, by taking care of their land, people would always have enough to eat.

Brodiaea bulb and flowers.

Maidu woman using a seed beater to knock seeds into a larger collecting basket.

Seed Cakes

Everywhere in the world, people eat lots of roots, green vegetables, nuts, berries, and especially seeds. Seeds are very important to humans. Even today, many of our favorite foods come from seeds: wheat (from which we make flour for breads) and rice, for example, are seeds of different grasses. We also use sunflower seeds, sesame seeds, mustard seeds, and others.

To the Indian people, the seeds of various grasses and wildflowers were also very important. They would watch their meadows carefully; when the plants began to dry and the seeds ripen, people would go out into the meadows with baskets to collect a rich harvest. Often families had special meadows to which they would return, year after year.

The Indian women treated their seed meadows with great care. When collecting seeds, they made sure that they left behind enough so that the meadow would be reseeded and there would be enough plants for the next year. They also made certain not to take too much so that the animals and birds would have enough food as well.

After they had gathered their seed crops, they would often set their meadows on fire, to keep them healthy. The fire burned away the brush that might otherwise overshadow the meadow grasses and wildflowers. The fire left behind a bed of ashes that fertilized the soil. The fire helped get rid of plants the native people didn't like, and it encouraged those they valued the most.

Nowadays, people work hard to get the land to grow seeds. We plow fields, pull out weeds, and add fertilizers. Native people made careful use of fire to accomplish many of the same things. They knew how to use fire well, how to burn so that the fire would do good and not harm the land. Fire was one of their most important tools for managing the land.

The Beautiful Tree

Acorns are a wonderful food and everywhere in California people used to eat them. Acorns grow on oak trees. There are many different kinds of oaks, each with its own kind of acorn. People especially loved acorns from the tanoak and black oak. Acorns were eaten often, in some places every day, the way we might eat bread.

Today Indian people no longer use acorns in their everyday meals. Like most other people in California, Indian people eat bread or tortillas, rice or potatoes. But on special occasions, people still make acorn soup. They make it for ceremonies or for parties (called "big times") when lots of people get together. Sometimes when someone is sick, you might see the mother or grandmother make a bowl of acorn soup. "Here," the grandmother says, "Have some of this. It's good for you."

Essie Parrish, who was a leading shaman or spiritual doctor for the Kashaya Pomo people, once talked about her feelings for the tanoak tree that provided such wonderful food.

In our language, we call the tanoak *chishkale*; it means "the Beautiful Tree." It's beautiful to look at. I never get tired of seeing it; it always lifts up my heart and makes me feel good. Every time when I go about the country to doctor the people who call me to them, that tree, when I see it for the first time, lets me know I'm home, and I feel good. Those who grow up here on my reservation, grow up with that tree also. It's like a relative or a good friend. It may sound funny to the white people, but that tree is beautiful because it gives us good food, and it's sweet too. I'm always happy when it's acorn picking time; I don't know how to explain it better than that. Long ago it was our most common food; we ate it every day. We stored up as much as we could. I guess that's why the people in the olden days gave that tree this name, "beautiful."

Acorn Soup

But acorn soup and acorn bread are not easy to make. It takes a lot of work and a lot of skill. You can't just collect acorns and throw them into a pot. First you have to gather them at the right time of year, when they are still fresh and before the deer or bears or bugs eat them. Then you have to dry them and crack and skin them. Then you pound them in a mortar and pestle to get flour. You then run lots of water through the flour to get the bitterness out. And even then you are not done! Now you have to cook the acorns. In the old days Indian people found a marvellous way to do this. They put acorn flour into a basket with some water, and then dropped large, red-hot rocks into the basket, stirring them around. The basket was so finely woven that nothing would leak out, and the hot rocks would bring the mixture to a boil. Within a very short time, they had wonderful acorn soup!

Some people, like the Yurok woman Bertha Peters in this 1993 photo, still know how to make acorn soup the old way. Here Bertha is stirring hot rocks in a basket full of acorn soup, using a wooden paddle, just as people have done for hundreds of years.

Granaries

People collected acorns each fall, and they then had to store them for the rest of the year. They sometimes stored them in big baskets that they kept in the house, other times in specially built structures called granaries.

ABOVE: Sierra Mewuk granaries, 1906.
OPPOSITE, LEFT: The Chemehuevi built granaries on top of their houses!
OPPOSITE, RIGHT: Cahuilla granary.
OPPOSITE, BELOW: Pomo granary, 1922.

59

Fishing Laws

In the old days, California had so many different places to fish. One group might fish in the ocean, another in a river, another might have a lake, another small streams, and yet another might fish in a calm bay. And there were so many different kinds of fish. Indian people everywhere developed a way to fish that was just right for the place where they lived and what they were fishing for.

Some people fished from boats using nets. Others had nets that they threw out from the land. Some people used harpoons; some used big hooks attached to poles, reaching under rocks to snag tasty eels; and some used a hook and line. When fishing in small streams, people learned that if they crushed certain roots and threw them in the water, the fish would get kind of "drunk" and float to the surface where they could easily be caught.

In northwestern California, the Yurok, Hupa, Karuk, and others built a kind of dam (called a weir) part of the way across the river to catch salmon.

People loved to fish. But in fishing, as in everything that Indians did, rules had to be followed. People had to make certain that they did not waste any fish, and that they did not catch so many that the number of fish would dwindle. That way, people felt, they would not only have plenty of fish for one season; they would have plenty of fish forever, or at least as long as the rules were followed.

Lucy Thompson, a Yurok woman who lived in the early 1900s, once described some of the rules that people had when fishing.

When the fish dam is put in, my people have very strict laws governing it. Families come in the morning, and each one takes from the fish trap what belongs to them and takes only as many salmon as they need. They dip out fish with a special net, and they must not let a single one go to waste. They must take care of all they take or suffer the penalty of the law, which was strictly enforced. After everyone gets their salmon, they use some fresh and the rest they cut up, smoke lightly, and dry.

In these traps at the dam, there gets to be a mass of salmon, so full that they make the whole structure of the fish dam quiver and tremble with their weight, by holding the water from passing through the lattice-work freely. After all have taken what they want of the salmon, which must be done in the early part of the day, an official opens the upper gates of the traps and lets the salmon pass on up the river, and at the same time great numbers are passing through the open gap left on the south side of the river. This is done so that the Hupas on up the Trinity River have a chance at the salmon catching. But they keep a close watch to see that there are enough left to effect the spawning, by which the supply is kept up for the following year.

A Hupa fishing dam, 1906.

Fishing in Northern California

OPPOSITE, LEFT: Josie Brown Marks (Yurok) cooking dried fish, 1928.
OPPOSITE, RIGHT: Little Ike (Karuk) fishing from a platform, probably before 1910.
OPPOSITE, BELOW: A Hupa man fishing at a trout dam, 1923.
RIGHT: Merk Oliver (Yurok) mending a fishing net, 1988.
BELOW: Frank Howe (Modoc) fishing from a boat, 1907.

A Great Hunter

Hunting has always been an important part of California Indian life. Just as cattle provide modern people with meat, leather for shoes, milk, and other goods, the animal world supplied Indians with much of what they needed.

The most popular animal to be hunted has always been deer. Deer meat (venison, as it is called) is still eaten, especially at ceremonies and get-togethers. In the old days, when a deer was killed, the meat would be divided among many people. The skin would be used to make clothing, the hooves to make musical instruments, and certain bones were used to make sharp-pointed tools (awls) for basketweaving. Even the brains were used—for tanning hides.

There were many different ways to hunt deer. Sometimes people had a deer drive, when a whole line of people chased the deer toward hunters who would be waiting with bows and arrows. Sometimes people hunted deer with nets which they would spread out across favorite deer trails and then chase the deer toward the nets. Another way of hunting took a lot of skill. A man would first spend time in a sweat-house sweating and rubbing his body with special plants to get rid of the human smell. Then he would put a deer mask over his head and go out after deer. When he saw a herd of deer, he would begin to move like a deer. When the deer looked up, he too would look up. When the deer moved away, he would move with them. Slowly he would move closer and closer to the deer. When he was so close that he could almost touch the deer, then he would fire his arrow. That way he seldom missed. It was surely a wonderfully exciting way to hunt.

Here a Pomo woman recalled how her grandfather used to hunt.

My grandfather was a great hunter. One time I saw him making traps for all kinds of birds like larks and quails and cottontails. He used to make old-time traps. He used to put lots of them out in the evening. He used to have baskets and filled them up with rabbits and birds. He used to have all of them in the traps and early the next morning he would go out to get them. And when he brought them home in the morning, he used to build a fire and take all the feathers off. He cleaned all the birds and cooked them. He was the only one who cooked them. None of us helped with that. And when we ate the bird, we never bit it or broke the bone. We just pulled the meat off. It would have given him have bad luck if we bit or broke the bones. That's the way we did things. He used to cook it on the coals.

My grandfather said he would put the deer head on when he wanted to go out hunting. He used to go out among the deer. The deer always wanted to smell him. He would just turn around and sit down. It used to make me laugh when he told that story.

Hupa man hunting with deer decoy mask so that the deer will let him get close to them.

Giving to the Deer

Hunting was done with great skill and much care. The animal that was hunted had to be treated respectfully. The meat would have to be received with gratitude. It was felt that the animals would avoid a hunter who treated them badly, and the hunter would have bad luck. As David Peri, a Coast Miwok man who lives in Sonoma County explains, hunters had many rules to follow, laws to obey.

The hunters "got up with the deer," ate no food, nor drank water; this was the second day of their fast. Should they get hungry, they ate the foods eaten by the deer: tender grass, new leaves, and blossoms. But they drank no water until they had given the deer they had taken the first drink of cool, fresh water, carried on a young leaf and placed in the deer's mouth. The two days of fasting, drinking only Indian tea, and bathing twice daily served to almost fade their "man smell" away, and lessen their chances of being detected by the deer. It also made their minds and bodies sensitive to all that they would experience on the hunt.

These people also thought differently about deer and hunting. They didn't *kill* deer, they *took* them. And they didn't take them for themselves, they took them for their families and relatives, and shared with their friends. In fact, those who came home with a deer didn't eat any of the meat. The hunters would only eat that brought back by others, never their own. It was not for themselves that they hunted; it was always for someone else. By not eating the meat from his own hunt, the hunter gave back the life that he had taken. This was called "Giving to the Deer." That is, a man became a hunter to take the deer's life in order that someone else would live, and make possible other lives.

Many Relatives

What a beautiful land the Indians of California lived in! It was full of so many different kinds of animals, birds, fish, and plants. In some places where there were great rivers, salmon in huge numbers came to lay their eggs. Sometimes the salmon run was so thick that it looked as if the river was entirely full of these magnificent fish.

Other places had great marshes that spread out for miles and miles. Here, every fall and winter, came millions of ducks and geese. They filled the air, sometimes almost blocking out the sun so that a big shadow would fall on the land until the flock had passed by. They settled into the marshes and swamps and the beating of their wings and their honking and quacking made a great noise.

On open meadows you might find herds of pronghorn antelope running. If you stood along the ocean beaches you might look out and watch great families of whales pass by, spouting into the air. If you went into the woods or along the streams you might find big grizzly bears. If you looked into the sky maybe you would see bald eagles or even condors.

Not all these animals lived at the same place. Each animal likes a particular kind of place, or environment, as it is called. There were many different environments in California, and each environment had its own kind of animals and plants, and the people there had learned how to best live in that kind of land. Yet, wherever they lived, native people loved their land and all its creatures. In fact they felt that the plants and animals, even the rocks and the streams, were a form of life not very different from people. All creation, they felt, was like a family. Here Lucy Smith, a respected Pomo basketweaver and elder, recalls what her mother taught her.

We had many relatives and we all had to live together; so we better learn how to get along with each other. My mother said it wasn't too hard to do. It was just like taking care of your younger brother or sister. You got to know them, find out what they liked and what made them cry, so you'd know what to do. If you took good care of them you didn't have to work as hard. Sounds like it's not true, but it is. When that baby gets to be a man or woman they're going to help you out.

You know, I thought she was talking about us Indians and how we are supposed to get along. I found out later from my older sister that mother wasn't just talking about Indians, but the plants, animals, birds—everything on this earth. They are our relatives and we better know how to act around them.

Lucy Smith with her daughter, Kathleen Smith, 1995.

4

Skills and Arts

Jennifer Bates (Sierra Mewuk) making a basket, about 1992.

People of Many Skills

California Indians have always been ingenious in their ability to make everything they needed from the materials around them.

Consider, for example, rocks and stones. To most people today, a rock or a stone is not very interesting or useful. But native people knew better. From hard stones, like obsidian and flint, they made knives and arrowheads. From soft stones like soapstone they carved bowls and pipes. From stones such as granite they made mortars and pestles with which to pound acorns, or weights that they could attach to fishing nets.

Bones of deer were made into awls for making baskets, or saws for cutting tule reeds. Plant fibers were worked into string and rope. Wood had a hundred uses: bows, arrows, paddles for stirring soup, looped sticks for lifting hot rocks out of cooking baskets, dice for playing games, and many more.

Even elk antler had many uses. People knew how to make wedges for splitting wood out of the antler, even how to make beautiful treasure boxes and decorated spoons.

These are just a few of the things that California Indians knew how to make to provide themselves with a comfortable and beautiful life.

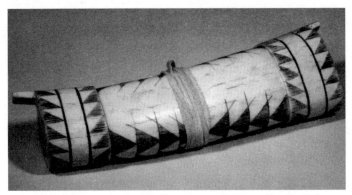

Elk antler purse for "Indian money" (dentalia shells) made by George Blake (Hupa/Yurok) in 1989.

Clothing

Stormy Rojas, 1993. This Yurok girl is wearing a traditional basketry cap and a ceremonial dress made of deerskin and shell. The shells jingle when she walks, and these dresses are admired almost as much for their music as for their looks.

When newcomers first came here, they felt that the Indians weren't wearing the right kind of clothing. The newcomers thought that the Indians weren't wearing as much clothing as they should, and it wasn't in the right style.

Yet each group of people had clothing that suited themselves and the kind of place where they lived. In the wintertime when people needed warm clothing, they wore wonderful fur blankets and cloaks. A favorite in many parts of California was the rabbit-skin blanket. It was made by getting a lot of rabbit skins and tanning them so that the leather was soft. Long strips were cut out of each skin and then twisted around so that they looked like long, fur-covered ropes. These strands of fur were then woven together to make a blanket that was soft and warm. In the summertime when it was hot, people wore much less clothing.

RIGHT: Drawing of an Ohlone woman from the Monterey Bay area, 1791. She is wearing a rabbit-skin cape and a tule skirt with a deer-skin coverlet.
BELOW: Pomo women dancers at a big time at D-Q University, 1995. Today at ceremonies and dances, Indian women from north central California often wear long dresses, sometimes deco-rated with ribbons, and old-style feather headdresses.

Making a Basket

What beautiful baskets people had in the old days! And so many baskets, too. There were baskets that were used as pots, as plates, as bowls, as cups, as hats, as special boxes for treasured jewelry. There were huge baskets that were used to store dried acorns and other foods, and the tiniest of baskets that were given as gifts. There were baskets that were used to gather seeds; baskets that were used to trap fish, birds, and other animals; and basketry cradles that made a comfortable and safe place for a baby to sleep. An old-fashioned Indian family might have had dozens of baskets.

Some baskets were woven so tightly that they could hold water. Some were decorated with interesting patterns, or even little beads and feathers. It was mostly women who made baskets, and while some were much better at it than others, nearly every woman was a skilled basketweaver. It took a long time to make a basket, sometimes months. It took a lot of skill and knowledge and constant work, but it was pleasant work.

People made baskets out of many different kinds of materials. They used roots of some plants and shoots or stems of others. The basketweaver didn't just go out into the woods and cut her materials at any old time or any old way. She gathered her materials at a certain season and in such a way that the plant was not injured, but actually made healthier! When weaving, the basketweaver felt that the materials she gathered were happy to be made into a basket. People felt they were working together with plants to make beautiful baskets and keep plants healthy. They felt that this is what people do in the world—they keep the world around them healthy and beautiful.

Vivien Hailstone (Yurok/Hupa/Karuk), 1982.

Baskets

ABOVE: A Hupa basket hat.

BELOW: A Karuk lidded basket by Elizabeth Hickox.

ABOVE: A Yokuts basket with rattlesnake design.

BELOW: A Pomo feathered basket.

Houses of the Sea

There were many, many different kinds of boats in California.

The Yurok, Tolowa, Hupa, and Karuk Indians are among those who had dugout canoes. They would get a big redwood log and carve it out with their tools. To make their work easier they would light a fire in the part of the log they were working on, then they would chip at the softer, burned part. In this way they made a beautifully shaped boat. Rivers were almost like highways, with people moving up and down stream in boats, to fish or trade or just to have a good time.

In other places people made boats out of tule reeds. Some people, like the Ohlone, used to go out into the San Francisco Bay on these canoe-shaped boats. Other people, such as some of the Yokuts groups of the San Joaquin Valley, used to make big barges by weaving tules around a frame of thin willow poles.

The Chumash and Tongva people of southern California made still another kind of boat. They cut redwood logs into planks or boards, which they then sewed together. In the cracks between the planks they put tar so that the boat wouldn't leak. They sanded the boats down until the redwood shined, and they embedded bits of shell into the wood for decoration.

Why were there so many different kinds of boats? People living in different places had different materials. They also had different kinds of waters. Some wanted boats to go out into the rough ocean, some wanted boats to go out into the calm bays or lakes, others wanted boats to go down fast-flowing rivers. Each people took the materials they had available, figured out what they needed, and learned to make the boats that were just right for them.

Fernando Librado, a Chumash man, once described the plank canoes of the Santa Barbara area.

The board canoe was the house of the sea. It was more valuable than a house on land and was worth much money.

Only a rich man owned such a canoe, and sometimes he might own several. With their tools the Indians were united in spirit. The old-time people had good eyes, and they would just look at a thing and see if it was right. No one hurried them up. The Indians wanted to build good canoes and they did not care how long it would take. An old canoemaker would have his helpers and he would allow no one else around. There was much to know. They knew all the secrets in order to make a canoe which was agile on the sea. When they finished making them, they went to sea. One of the canoes was like a flower on the water.

This plank canoe was built by contemporary Chumash people and launched in 1988.

80

OPPOSITE, LEFT: Harry Holmes and his son-in-law, Dave Mitchell, with Dave Mitchell, Jr., on Clear Lake in a tule canoe called a "balsa."
OPPOSITE, BELOW: Mohave raft loaded with melons and squash, 1907.
RIGHT: A Hupa dugout canoe, 1923.
BELOW: A Yurok dugout canoe, outfitted with a sail, crossing the Klamath River, about 1926.

David Smith (Pomo), 1989.

Songs

People everywhere in the world have music. Everyone, everywhere has songs.

In the old days, just about everyone knew many songs. Some songs might be lighthearted or funny. Some might make you feel strong and really good inside. Some songs might help a person express sadness or anger. Some might help give a person a religious experience. A song might help focus the mind of a man so he could hunt better, or a song might keep a woman company while she wove a basket. A song might be so powerful it could chase away sickness or unhappiness.

Where do songs come from? Sometimes, it seems, a song just comes to you. This is how many Indian people have always felt about certain songs. It is as if the song were a being, and it came to a person, almost like an animal might come to a person. The song was thought of as a living thing that would allow itself to be sung. Some songs belonged to particular people. They were like property, and no one else could sing them without permission of the owner.

Traditional songs are still sung by many people. They are sung by people playing games, like the hand game, for example, when each player brings along his or her best and most powerful songs. They are part of ceremonies, when a line of singers creates the tune to which the dancers move. Storytellers often sing, when one of the characters in their story sings a song. And then there are long songs, like the bird songs of southern California, which are sung for four nights in a row. The bird songs tell the story of magical beings that made great journeys over the land before people were created on the earth. In the old days, singers would begin the bird songs when it got dark and sing all night until it got light. Then the next day, when it got dark, they would continue. What powerful memories these singers had! Today there are still people who know the bird songs, the lightning songs, and many other songs that tell great stories and recount the history of very ancient times.

Most Indian songs cannot be translated into English very well: you have to hear them in their original language to catch the rhythm and hear the music of their original words. Here, though, are two shorter songs translated into English, to give you an idea of the variety of California Indian songs.

Here is a gentle Wintu love song, once sung by a man named Harry Marsh.

Before you go over the snow-mountain to the north,
Downhill toward the north,
Oh me, do look back at me.

You who dwell below the snow-mountain,
Do look back at me.

This fierce Wintu song, once sung by a woman named Fanny Brown, would be used to magically harm enemies.

To the edge of the earth
To the edge of the earth
To the edge of the earth
Snap all the people!
Snap all the people!
To the edge of the earth
To the edge of the earth!

Singing has always been an important part of California Indian life. Here James Donohue (Yurok), Julian Lang (Karuk), and Merk Oliver (Yurok) sing while playing a game of "Indian cards," 1990.

Dance

In the old days almost any occasion was a time for dancing. There was dancing just for the fun of it, when people would get together, some singing and playing instruments, and some dancing. It was a wonderful way of bringing people together.

There were also more serious dances. A traditional doctor or healer danced to help cure someone. People danced together to encourage the acorns or other plants to grow. They danced to give thanks for a good harvest, they danced to celebrate a victory after war. Throughout California people still dance. It is one of the favorite ways of getting together.

While some dancing is just for fun, much of it is for religious purposes. Dance is felt to be a form of prayer; by dancing people pray with their whole bodies. In northwestern California, for example, people still hold a ten-day dance called the Jump Dance every fall. They feel that these dances put the world into balance, and put people back into balance with the world. This is people's work: to balance the world, to fix it, to use dance to make the world whole and healthy again. It is very important work, and many Indian people still take it very seriously.

In some places a new kind of dance is developing. It is pow-wow dancing, and it was brought to California by Indians who moved here from other states. It has a strong drum beat and very colorful feathers and dance outfits and lots of really fancy steps. Many California Indians like these dances: they are such fun and so beautiful. Others, however, like the old kind of California Indian dances much better. Some don't like to dance at all. There really isn't just one way to be Indian, is there?

Lake County Pomo dancer.

Today the modern and the traditional mix in surprising and creative ways. Many California Indians are moving into new media, such as painting and sculpture, often bringing with them an older way of looking at the world. This painting is by Kathleen Smith (Coast Miwok/Southern Pomo).

5

An Alive and Sacred World

Fanny Flounder, a Yurok traditional healer who practiced around 1900.

These Baskets are Alive

There is an old way of thinking among California Indians, still deeply felt, that everything in the world is alive in the same way humans are alive. Deer, salmon, acorns, rocks, streams, the sun—everything—has life! Everything has thoughts, power, feelings, memory. Everything is a kind of person. And to get along in a world like this takes care, understanding, and religious awareness.

For California Indians, religion means much more than going to church once a week or having certain beliefs. Especially in the old days, and even today, religion is very much a part of every-day life. Even something as down-to-earth as gathering basketry materials is seen as religious. Norma Turner, a Mono basket-weaver, describes what it is like to collect materials, and how she feels about a basket once it is made.

I like to go out and just take my time, and I pray and I get closer to my Creator out there. And it's just a real closeness when you get out and start doing what, you know, was provided for. We never go out without thanking our Creator for providing us with whatever kind of material we're getting.

I don't know what I'd do if I had to sell one of those big cooking baskets. They're a part of the family. They're just like one of the children. And these baskets are alive. These baskets, just like the rocks are alive. These materials that we make baskets with are alive. There's a connection between the ancestors, the people, the basketmakers, and these baskets.

All Things Are People

Because everything is alive, everything has history—a story of how things came to be what they are today. Among California Indian people there is a belief that before the present age, before the time of humans, another world once existed here. In this world were divine beings, a kind of people with names like Coyote, Bear, Sun, Moon, Fog, Flint, and Gopher. These people lived together and did the sorts of things that ordinary people do: they loved each other, fought each other, and often tricked each other. They hunted, gambled, raised children, and usually had magical powers. By their actions they shaped the world, creating the rules by which humans would later live.

As the age of these divinities drew to a close, there came a period of "transformation." Now the divinity named Coyote turned into the animal, coyote; the being named Sun rose into the heavens to become the sun; the acorn maidens dropped their human form to become acorns. Yet while they took on their current forms, the things of the world were still divine beings, still alive and powerful. To live in this world, people have to know about them, know how to treat them, know their history. That is the purpose of myths: to tell the history of the beings around us so that everyone will know how to behave.

One story of how the acorns got to be what they are today was told by the Karuk people. There are so many different kinds of oak trees, each with a different kind of acorn. Some of these acorns have caps that look smooth, some of them have caps that look rough. Some make delicious soup, some not. How did this come about?

Once, Acorns were Spirit-people. They were told, "You will soon have to leave the Spirit world. You are going to Earth. You must all have nice hats to wear. You will have to weave them." So they started to weave good-looking hats.

Then all at once they were told, "You will have to leave now. Go quickly." Black Oak Acorn did not have time to finish her hat, so she picked up her big bowl basket. Tan Oak Acorn did not have time to clean her hat and make it smooth. But Post Oak Acorn and Maul Oak Acorn finished their hats perfectly, and even had time to clean them. Tan Oak Acorn noticed this, and said: "Though my hat is not clean, I will be the best acorn soup."

Then they left. They spilled from the Heavens into humans' world. "Humans will spoon us up," they said. They were Spirit-people, those Acorn Maidens. They shut their eyes and then they turned their faces into their hats when they came to this earth. That is the way the Acorns did.

Tan Oak Acorn wished bad luck toward Post Oak Acorn and Maul Oak Acorn because they had nice hats. She was jealous of them. Today nobody likes to eat Post Oak Acorn. And Maul Oak Acorn does not taste good either. They do not taste good and their soups are black.

When they spilled down from the Heavens, they turned their faces into their hats. And nowadays they still have their faces inside their hats.

Tan Oak Acorn did not have time to clean her hat and make it smooth.

Black Oak Acorn picked up her big bowl.

Maul Oak Acorn finished her hat out perfectly.

93

Sun and Moon

Sometimes people think of myths as lies. The word "myth" is often used that way. When we say, "That's just a myth," we often mean, "That's not quite true."

But actually myths do tell truths—truths so big and so important that sometimes they can only be told through stories. What, for example, are some of the truths behind the myth of the acorn maidens that we just read? Perhaps by pointing out that those acorns with the most well-finished caps taste the worst, the myth is trying to tell us that good looks can be deceptive, a very important lesson indeed! Perhaps it is also trying to tell us that traits such as pride, jealousy, and a desire to be useful are not just human characteristics but are part of the world around us as well—something that even acorns feel. This sense that everything in the world feels, thinks, and acts in a humanlike fashion is a very important part of what myths try to teach us. They present a world to us in which everything responds the way humans respond: sometimes with wisdom, sometimes with petty jealousy, sometimes foolishly, sometimes with wondrous beauty. Trees, rocks, moon, sun, rivers, deer, fish, birds—all things in the world—behave like humans. To understand this well is to understand something very important and beautiful. It makes the world fuller and richer. That is what myths do best: they make the world fuller and richer, and they make being a human a lot less lonely.

How wonderful it must be to look into the sky and see the sun and the moon not as lifeless objects, but as a kind of people. According to the Maidu they were sister and brother, who once lived in a house just like people do now. They had to move into the heavens because their house developed a little problem— a problem very familiar to many people.

Sun and Moon were sister and brother. They did not rise at first. Many different animals were sent to try and see if they could make the two rise, but failed. None of them could get into the house in which the brother and sister lived. This house was of solid stone, and was far away to the east.

At last Gopher and Angle-Worm went. Angle-Worm made a tiny hole, boring down outside, and coming up inside the house. Gopher followed, carrying a bag of fleas. He opened it, and let half of the fleas out. They bit the brother and sister so that they moved from the floor where they were to the sleeping-platform. Then Gopher let out the rest of the fleas, and these made life so miserable for Sun and Moon that they decided to leave the house. The sister did not want to travel by night, so the brother said he would go then, and became the Moon. The sister travelled by day, and became the Sun.

Drawing of the sun, based on Chumash rock art, by Nashun Huaute (Chumash).

Creating a World

Myths are stories that explain many important things: how the world was made long ago; how people first came into being; how different animals and plants, rivers, rocks, and mountains were formed; and why things are done the way they are done today. Through the telling of myths people are able to pass on their history and their knowledge of the world around them.

Every people, throughout the world, has a myth that tells how the world came to be and how people were made. In this Maidu creation myth, Earth-maker climbs down a rope from the sky and meets Turtle. Turtle is floating on the water in a raft along with a mysterious being named Pehe-ipe. Turtle and Earth-maker decide on a simple plan to make some good dry land.

In the beginning there was no sun, no moon, no stars. All was dark, and everywhere there was only water. A raft came floating on the water, and in it were two persons—Turtle and Pehe-ipe. Then from the sky a rope of feathers was let down. And down the rope came Earth-maker. His face was covered and was never seen, but his body shone like the sun. He sat down for a long time and said nothing.

At last Turtle said, "Where do you come from?" and Earth-maker answered, "I come from above." Then Turtle said, "Brother, can you not make for me some good dry land, so that I may sometimes come up out of the water?" Earth-maker replied, "I don't know. You want to have some dry land? Well, how am I going to get any earth to make it?" Turtle answered, "If you will tie a rock about my left arm, I'll dive for some." Earth-maker took the end of a rope and tied it to Turtle. Turtle said, "If the rope is not long enough, I'll just jerk it once, and you must haul me up; if it is long enough, I'll give two jerks, and then you must pull me up quickly, as I shall have all the earth that I can carry."

Turtle was gone six years and when he came up, he was covered with green slime, he had been down so long. When he reached the top of the water, the only earth he had was a very little bit under his nails. The rest had all washed away. Earth-maker took a stone knife and carefully scraped the earth out from under Turtle's nails. He put the earth in the palm of his hand, and rolled it about until it was round and as large as a small pebble. He laid it on the stern of the raft.

By and by he went to look at it: it had not grown at all. The third time that he went to look at it, it had grown so that it could not be spanned by the arms. The fourth time he looked, it was big as the world. The raft was aground, and all were mountains as far as he could see. The raft came ashore at Tadoiko, and the place can be seen today.

After the land was created, Earth-maker created plants and animals. "Kodoyampeh and Creation of Plants and Animals" is an interpretation of the Maidu creation story by Maidu artist Harry Fonseca, painted about 1991.

Sacred Houses

LEFT: Modern Sierra Mewuk
roundhouse at Tuolumne
Rancheria.
BELOW: Cahuilla ceremonial
house, 1924 or earlier.
OPPOSITE: In many parts of
California there are special houses
where religious dances and
ceremonies are held. In this picture
a man in a long, feathered cloak
stands in front of an underground
Wintun roundhouse, 1906.

98

A Tale of Coyote

Everywhere in North American myths, there is someone like Coyote. Coyote is called the "trickster." Some of the names that other peoples have for the trickster are The Foolish One, The Great Rabbit, Hare, Raven, and Glooscap. But in California, the trickster took his name from the small, doglike animal who hung around the edges of the villages, hunting gophers, nosing through piles of garbage, and occasionally stealing salmon and deer meat from the drying racks.

Coyote represents a little of everything, and often all at once: good and bad, foolish and crafty, creative and unimaginative, ridiculous and godlike. Stories about him are often so hilarious and absurd that they appeal to everyone, young and old. These stories not only bring people together for a good time of listening and laughter, but they have important moral lessons as well.

In a typical Coyote story, such as this one told by a Wintu named Jo Bender, our "hero" sets off on a funny mission and quickly gets into trouble. And at the end, as he so often does, he tries to convince everyone he was in no trouble at all.

Coyote was going up the river to visit someone. He was very well dressed. He had his quiver, bow and arrows, moccasins and beads. He looked very fine. It was a hot summer day. He came to a nice stretch of sand. He saw Bullfish sunning himself. He was black as charcoal. Coyote said, "What are you doing there?"

Bullfish didn't say a word. Coyote talked and talked but Bullfish never answered. At last Coyote said, "You are pretty small. You are too little to do anything. You're so small, I'll bet you can't swallow my toe," and at the same time he thrust his toe in front of Bullfish's mouth. Bullfish just turned his head away.

Then Coyote said, "I'll give you my bow and arrows if you bite me." He teased Bullfish that way for a long time. Finally Bullfish nipped Coyote's toe. Coyote did not pay any attention to him; he only continued to taunt him. Soon Bullfish had swallowed Coyote's leg; Coyote became frightened and begged for mercy, but Bullfish ignored him and kept on swallowing him. Coyote offered him all his fine things, but Bullfish just swallowed him entirely and swam off under a rock in the riffle.

The people missed Coyote. They hunted for him and found his valuables on the sand and saw the track where he had been dragged in. So they asked a doctor to find out where he was. The doctor went into a trance and about in the middle of the night said that Coyote was under the water, that Bullfish had swallowed him, and that he was not yet dead.

Then Bullfish made the water muddy so the people could not find him. Otter, Raccoon, everyone looked for Coyote but they could not find him. At last Mud-Spear [a water bird] climbed a tree and looked. He said, "I see a tail under a rock in the riffle. I am going to try to spear him." So he took a spear pole, aimed carefully, and speared Bullfish right above the tail. The people pulled Bullfish out and cut open his stomach. Coyote jumped out and said, "Nephew, I have been sleeping."

Coyote by Harry Fonseca (Maidu).

Dance and Have a Good Time
So the Earth Will Feel Good

Today many Indians are Catholics, Mormons, Baptists, or members of other churches. They feel that these churches offer them much knowledge and insight and they feel good about their religious beliefs.

Some Indian people find ways to combine the traditions of their church with the old ways of believing, while still others would rather stay with the old ways exclusively. They still live in a world in which everything around them is full of power and holiness and religious history. They like the beliefs, dances, prayers, and songs that their parents, grandparents, and ancestors have known. It gives them strength, wisdom, and power, and they feel an aspect of truth that they cannot get elsewhere.

In northwestern California, among the Yurok, Karuk, Hupa, Tolowa, and other people, religious ceremonies are still a major part of people's lives. Each year, for example, people still perform the great dances that are needed to "fix the world"—to repair the damage done to the world during the year, to root the world in place so that it will be secure and stable. Julian Lang, a modern Karuk, describes the feelings that go into such a ceremony.

We are fixing the Earth. Tonight is the dark of the moon, the beginning of our new year. The Medicine Prayer Man will stand up before all the people, a symbol of strength and good thoughts. For days now he has been fasting and sweating himself in the Best Sweat-house known in our world. Each day he walks along the ancient trails to the fire places, where he sweeps the Earth clean of all sickness and prays for abundant food, water-food, and walks-in-the-mountain food. For days we have been shooting our arrows, piercing the Earth, waking it up so the Medicine Man's prayers will be heard. So, our prayers will be heard likewise.

Traditional people of northwestern California believe that the great dances that bring balance to the earth are the most important thing that people do in this world. One of these is called the Jump Dance. The photos on this page show the dancers in beautiful headdresses that are made partly of bright red woodpecker feathers.

ABOVE: A dance at the Yurok town of Requa. RIGHT: Dancers at the Yurok town of Pecwan, 1893.

103

One of our oldest women said to me last night, "You folks must dance and have a good time so the Earth will feel good." Tonight we will have three dances, and a feast. It is Indian New Year at the Center of the World tonight! We will all shake hands and say to each other, "We have fixed the Earth. We have reset the pole that makes the Earth hold fast."

When the Earth was created it was not known how Human was going to do, how Human was going to live. Finally the Spirit People knew Human must eat salmon, acorns, deermeat, and all kinds of plant and water food. The Ikxareeyavs, the Spirit Beings, said, "This is going to be your medicine. This will help you in the hunt. There are your tools. This is your Way." When the First People began to die, the Ikxareeyavs were shocked at such imbalance. They sat and talked. "Human must fix the Earth each year," they concluded. So, now we have our Ikxariya'áraar, our Spirit-Man (Medicine Man) who sweeps the world clean just as the Ikxareeyav did the first time. "Human must War Dance and White Deerskin Dance. That's how to keep away sickness and keep the Earth stable and in balance," the Ikxareeyav said. Tonight we will have finished doing as they once did so many generations ago. "That's the best way there is," our oldest woman said. "Do like they did and you can't go wrong."

6

Modern Times

Bun Lucas, a Pomo elder, artist, and religious leader, carving a bear, about 1992.

Recent History

For many thousands of years California Indian cultures flourished. Then, a little more than two hundred years ago, outsiders arrived and took control of the land away from the native people. Beginning in 1769, the Spanish began to set up missions, forts, and towns. The Spanish felt that they knew better than anyone else how to live in California. They felt that they knew how the Indians should dress, how they should gather food, and what they should think about religion. They thought that native people should be like *they* were, should live like the white Europeans. They thought that people shouldn't eat acorns or wild seeds but rather should have farms and grow wheat and other such foods. They thought that instead of hunting deer and antelope and rabbits, and instead of fishing for salmon, people ought to raise cattle and pigs and that they should eat that kind of food. And they thought that instead of having their own beliefs, Indian people ought to believe what the Europeans believed.

They thought that because the Indians did not think and act like them that they were bad and even stupid, and that Indians should be forced to work and forced to believe a certain way. They invited the Indians to come into the missions and once they were there, they felt they had the right to make them do things their way. If the Indians refused, the missionaries felt they had the right to send soldiers after them and punish them.

In the missions, many, many Indians caught new diseases that the Spaniards brought from Europe, and they died. Under the strict Spanish rules, many native people lost their beliefs, lost their languages, and lost many Indian ways of doing things.

The missions did not cover all of California, just the coastal areas, mostly in the south. It was not until 1849 and the Gold Rush that the rest of California was settled by newcomers. These were at first gold miners who came from other parts of the United States and from around the world. Once here, many of

This drawing of Mission San Carlos Borromeo (near Monterey) was drawn in 1786. It shows Indians, now dressed in cloth, lined up to watch the arrival of important French visitors.

them looked for land to farm. Others came to set up ranches, to open stores and hotels and other businesses in towns and cities, and to log and mine. Many of them did not like the Indian people they met here. They saw the Indians as different, and to them "different" was bad. The Indians had different languages, different ways of doing things, different colored skin. Many of the Americans who came here were very prejudiced, and some of them were vicious. Some of them went out and simply killed Indian people with their rifles. If the Indians didn't fight back they were called cowards who deserved to die. If they did fight back they were called savages and the army was called out to control them. No matter what they did, they were hated and pushed off their land.

Not everyone felt this way. There were many who became friends with the Indians, who helped them, and who learned from them. But there were many others who treated them badly.

There are many reasons why people are prejudiced, and they are complicated reasons. One thing that seemed to cause the prejudice against the Indians was the fact that the newcomers wanted Indian land. They wanted the places in the valleys and alongside the rivers where Indians had lived for thousands of years. They wanted these places for their homes. They wanted to make new farms and ranches in the meadows where the Indians had gathered food and hunted deer. They wanted the rivers to be dammed for power, and they wanted the forests to be cut for lumber. The Indians were in the way, and many of the new people hated them.

It was partly to get Indians out of the way, and partly to protect them from the newcomers who might murder them, that reservations were set up. Often reservations were pieces of land that Indians "reserved" from their original territory—small portions of their once large land holdings. Other times reservations were plots of land set aside by the government to provide

California Indians had to adapt to the ways of the newcomers. Here a Luiseño family sits outside an old-style brush dwelling. Next to it they have built, out of traditional materials, a new-style structure with a peaked roof.

Removed from the Land

Before the coming of Europeans, the Cupeño people lived in a beautiful desert area of southern California. Here they hunted deer and quail, and gathered acorns, seeds, and cactus fruits. They lived well and felt that their land had been theirs almost since the beginning of time.

Like other California Indian tribes, the Cupeños suffered from the diseases and troubles brought by the newcomers. But in time they adapted. Most of the Cupeños lived in a village of adobe houses which they had built. They planted farms and orchards. They even had a small schoolhouse for their children. They did everything they could to succeed in the new world, to adapt to its ways.

But in 1903 the U.S. government claimed that the land they were living on was not theirs, and sold it to a stranger. The Cupeños would have to leave their homes. On May 12, they were expelled from their land and moved by wagon train forty miles away to a place called Pala. Their homes were torn down and destroyed.

Thus the Cupeños, like many, many other California peoples, were removed from land that had always been theirs. Today, the Pala Reservation, the place to which they were moved, is the center of Cupeño tribal culture.

OPPOSITE, ABOVE: The ranch where the Cupeños lived before they were removed to a reservation. OPPOSITE, BELOW: The Cupeño wagon train camped for the night. RIGHT: Cupeños on the road during the removal from their homes to the reservation.

refuge for many different tribes. In California larger pieces of land were called reservations; smaller pieces of land were often called rancherias, and indeed they still are.

Reservation life was very difficult. The reservations were usually too small to support the numbers of people that were living on them, the land was often too dry or rocky to farm, and there were few ways of earning a living. Although the government promised schools and other services, these were often of very poor quality, and Indian people, especially in the nineteenth century, lived in miserable poverty.

Indians suffered dreadfully and the population dropped rapidly. Many people—even the Indians' friends—thought that soon Indians would be extinct. Many well-meaning people felt that for Indians to survive in this new country they would have to stop being Indians. They would have to live just like everyone else. So every attempt was made to get Indian people to stop speaking their own languages and to speak only English; to give up their old ways and to learn new ways; to give up their religion and their ceremonies; to go to schools and to get jobs.

As time passed, Indians have indeed become a lot more like the other people in America. They have had no choice but to wear ordinary clothes, speak English, go to schools, get jobs, and live in houses like most other people. Some, but not all, even liked the new life.

Others, though, have wanted to be more old-fashioned, and keep at least some of their old ways. Many young children, for example, might wear levis and play basketball and watch TV and go to a regular school, but on weekends they might still go to special dances with their parents. They might still eat acorn soup on special occasions. They might even be learning to sing some of the old songs or speak some words in their own language.

Indian people have suffered greatly over the last couple of hundred years. This is something to be sad about. They have

Hupa girls at boarding school, 1907.

also managed to survive! Many are eagerly learning about the old ways and they are passing their traditions on to their children. They are proud to be Indian, and they are happy to be alive. They are pleased to keep alive some of the ceremonies, some of the beliefs, some of the language. It gives them pleasure and it makes their lives better. They don't have just one culture, they have two cultures. They are still Indians, proud to have survived, and they expect to be here for a long time too.

Although it is true that many things have changed in the last two hundred years, many things have remained the same. Young Indian people throughout California are carrying on the old traditions.

LEFT: Paul Kusca (Yurok) demonstrating the Brush Dance, a dance for healing children, 1989. RIGHT: Carson Bates (Sierra Mewuk) making a brush from soaproot fibers and soaproot glue, 1994. BELOW: Amora Stevenot (Sierra Mewuk) helping to prepare acorn flour, 1994.

A Good Life to Look Forward to

People sometimes think of California Indian life as something in the past, but it isn't. It's very much alive today. And for some, like Rochelle Marie O'Rourke, a young mother and basketweaver, it is in the future as well.

Rochelle Marie O'Rourke (Tolowa/Yurok/Pit River) with her son, Mech, 1991.

I love [basketweaving]. You create something that is alive. You put your heart and spirit into it, and it's alive. Whatever's in you, you put into the basket.

It's part of my life, and I want it to be part of my kids' life too. I want them to live it, not just know it. I, too, need to live it, so that my children will live it. It can't go away. If it goes away, we go away. We die. There's no other way to explain it.

I want to weave baskets. I want it to be part of my cooking, of my eating, of my raising children. These baskets are utensils. I want to be using them every day. I like to see myself cooking acorns with baskets and rocks, with kids all around me, somewhere along the river. And someday when I'm an elder I want to put my grandchildren in baby baskets made by me. That's pretty neat. It's a good life to look forward to.

California Indian Resources

Lake County Museum
 255 North Forbes Street
 Lakeport, CA 95453
 (707) 263-4555

Marin Museum of the American Indian
 2200 Novato Boulevard
 Novato, CA 94947
 (415) 897-4064

Mendocino County Museum
 400 East Commercial Street
 Willits, CA 95490
 (707) 459-2736

Oakland Museum
 1000 Oak Street
 Oakland, CA 94607
 (510) 834-2413

Palm Springs Desert Museum
 101 Museum Drive
 Palm Springs, CA 92262
 (619) 325-7186

Phoebe Apperson Hearst Museum of
Anthropology
 103 Kroeber Hall
 University of Calif., Berkeley
 Berkeley, CA 94720
 (510) 642-3681

San Diego Museum of Man
 1350 El Prado, Balboa Park
 San Diego, CA 92101
 (619) 239-2001

Santa Barbara Museum of Natural
History
 2559 Puesta del Sol Rd.
 Santa Barbara, CA 93105
 (805) 682-4711

Southwest Museum
 234 Museum Drive
 Los Angeles, CA 90042
 (213) 221-2163

Trees of Mystery/End of the Trail
Indian Museum
 15500 Highway 101-N
 Klamath, CA 95548
 (707) 482-2251

Yosemite Museum
 Yosemite National Park, CA 95389
 (209) 372-0282

Publishers specializing in California Indian history and literature include **Heyday Books** (P.O. Box 9145, Berkeley, CA 94709), **Ballena Press** (Ballena Press Publishers' Services, P.O. Box 2510, Novato, CA 94948), and **Malki Press** (11-795 Fields Rd., Banning, CA 92220). The **University of California Press** and some other university presses, such as **University of New Mexico**, **University of Nebraska**, and **University of Oklahoma**, have also published books about California Indians.

PUBLICATIONS: *News from Native California* (P.O. Box 9145, Berkeley, CA 94709), *Journal of California and Great Basin Anthropology* (CSU Bakersfield, Dept. of Sociology and Anthropology, 9001 Stockdale Hwy., Bakersfield, CA 93311), *The Native* (7427 Braeridge Way, Sacramento, CA 95831), and *American Indian Culture and Resource Journal* (UCLA, 3220 Campbell Hall, 405 N. Hilgard Ave., Los Angeles, CA 90024-1548).

Text Credits

FAMILY. From Burt and Ethel Aginsky, *Deep Valley* (New York: Stein and Day, 1967), 18. The statement was narrated in 1935 by a man who was reputed to have been 112 years old.

CHILDHOOD GAMES. From Marie Potts, *The Northern Maidu* (Happy Camp, Calif.: Naturegraph Publishers, Inc., 1977), 22, 23, 45.

WHEN I WAS A CHILD. From Verne F. Ray, *Primitive Pragmatists: The Modoc Indians of Northern California* (Seattle: University of Washington Press, 1963), 107-109. As reprinted in *News from Native California* 4, no. 3 (1990), 12.

COYOTE AND THE ACORNS. From Jean Sapir, "Yurok Tales," *Journal of American Folklore* 41 (1928), 254. The story was told by Mrs. Haydom in the summer of 1927.

LEARNING TO HUNT. From Leslie Spier, "Southern Diegueño Customs," *University of California Publications in American Archaeology and Ethnology* 20 (1923), 336. Jim McCarthy was over eighty years old when he told this memory near present-day Campo in San Diego County, in 1920.

A GIRL'S DANCE SONG. From Stephen Powers, *Tribes of California* (Washington: U.S. Government Printing Office, 1877), 236.

BECOMING A MAN. From Susan Parks, *Samson Grant, Atsuge Shaman* (Redding, Calif.: Redding Museum and Art Center). As reprinted in *News from Native California* 1, no. 2 (1987), 4.

GETTING MARRIED. From Walter Goldschmidt, "Nomlaki Ethnography," *University of California Publications in American Archaeology and Ethnology* 42, no. 4 (1951), 377.

TARANTULA. From Edward W. Gifford, "Coast Yuki Myths," *Journal of American Folklore* 50 (1937), 170.

MANY KINDS OF PEOPLE. From William Wallace, "Personality Variation in Primitive Society," *Journal of Personality* 15 (1947), 321.

CHOOSING A CHIEF. From C. Darryl Forde, "Ethnography of the Yuma Indians," *University of California Publications in American Archaeology and Ethnology* 28 (1931), 135. Patrick Miguel gave this account in 1929, when he was in his early fifties.

TRAINING TO BE A WARRIOR. From Walter Goldschmidt, "Nomlaki Ethnography," *University of California Publications in American Archaeology and Ethnology* 42, no. 4 (1951), 341-342.

MESSENGERS. From Walter Goldschmidt, "Nomlaki Ethnography," *University of California Publications in American Archaeology and Ethnology* 42, no. 4 (1951), 342. Jeff Jones narrated this story in 1936 when he was 70 years old. A photo taken at the time shows him to have been a strikingly handsome and intelligent-looking man, with a great drooping mustache and laughing eyes.

TRADING. From Walter Goldschmidt, "Nomlaki Ethnography," *University of California Publications in American Archaeology and Ethnology* 42, no. 4 (1951), 337.

DOCTORING. From Robert Oswalt, "Kashaya Texts," *University of California Publications in Linguistics* 36, (1964), 223.

THE BEAUTIFUL TRAIL. From Cora Du Bois, "Wintu Ethography," *University of California Publications in American Archaeology and Ethnology* 36, no. 1 (1935), 79.

THE BEAUTIFUL TREE. From David W. Peri, "Plant of the Season: Oaks," *News from Native California* 1, no. 5 (1987), 9.

FISHING LAWS. From Lucy Thompson, *To the American Indian: Reminiscences of a Yurok Woman.* (Berkeley: Heyday Books, 1991), 177-178. Lucy Thompson was born in Pecwan in 1853, a woman (as she described herself) "of highest birth." Although English was not her first language, she wrote and self-published her remarkable book in 1916 to tell the truth about her people.

A GREAT HUNTER. From Elizabeth Colson, *Autobiographies of Three Pomo Women* (Berkeley: Archaeological Research Facility, Department of Anthropology, University of California at Berkeley, 1974), 129. The narrator, whose name is not revealed, was born in 1882 and dictated her reminiscences in 1941.

GIVING TO THE DEER. From David W. Peri, "Venison: Indian Beef, On Deer and Preparing Venison for Cooking or Why Things Are and How They Came to Be That Way," *News from Native California* 2, no.1 (1988), 15.

MANY RELATIVES. From David W. Peri and Scott M. Patterson, *Ethnobotanical Resources of the Warm Springs Dam-Lake Sonoma Project Area, Sonoma County, California* (San Francisco: U.S. Army Corps of Engineers, 1979). As reprinted in *News from Native California* 6, no. 2 (1992), 29.

HOUSES OF THE SEA. From Travis Hudson, Jan Timbrook, and Melissa Rempe, eds., "Tomol: Chumash Watercraft as Described in the Ethnographic Notes of John P. Harrington," *Ballena Press Anthropological Papers* 9 (1978). As reprinted in *News from Native California* 2, no. 4 (1988), 17.

SONGS:
> [WINTU LOVE SONG] From Dorothy Demetracopoulou, "Wintu Songs,"
> *Anthropos* 30 (1935), 492.
> [TO THE EDGE OF THE EARTH] From Dorothy Demetracopoulou, "Wintu
> Songs," *Anthropos* 30 (1935), 488. The song was recorded in 1929.

THESE BASKETS ARE ALIVE. From Bev Ortiz, "Interviews from CALIFORNIA
INDIAN BASKETWEAVERS GATHERING June 28-30, 1991," *News from Native
California* 6, no. 1 (1991), 26.

ALL THINGS ARE PEOPLE. From John P. Harrington, "Karuk Indian Myths,"
Bureau of American Ethnology, Bulletin 107 (1932), 6. As reprinted in *News
from Native California* 1, no. 4 (1987), 15.

SUN AND MOON. From Roland Dixon, "Maidu Myths," *Bulletin of the American
Museum of Natural History* 17 (1902), 78.

CREATING A WORLD. From Roland Dixon, "Maidu Myths," *Bulletin of the
American Museum of Natural History* 17 (1902), 39.

A TALE OF COYOTE. From Cora Du Bois and Dorothy Demetracopoulou,
"Wintu Myths," *University of California Publications in American Archaeology and Ethnology* 28 (1931), 383.

DANCE AND HAVE A GOOD TIME. From Julian Lang, "Peethivthaaneen," *News
from Native California* 6, no. 2 (1992), 17.

A GOOD LIFE TO LOOK FORWARD TO. From Rochelle Marie O'Rourke,
News from Native California 6, no. 1 (1991/92), 35. Recorded by Malcolm
Margolin.

Photo Credits

9   Coast Miwok singers at Kule Loklo, ca. 1990. Photo by Lee Brumbaugh.
11   Hupa house, 1890. Photo by Col. C.E. Woodruff. Courtesy of National
     Museum of the American Indian (Smithsonian Institution). Negative #11786.
11   Yurok sweat-house at Pecwan, date unknown. Courtesy of Phoebe Apper-
     son Hearst Museum of Anthropology. Negative #15-3829.
12   Central California house and granary, ca.1853. Drawing by Henry B. Brown.
     Courtesy of The Bancroft Library.
12   Pomo tule house at Clear Lake, July 1917. Photographer unknown. Courtesy
     of The Bancroft Library.
13   Cahuilla house, date unknown. Courtesy of Southwest Museum. Negative
     #18,703.
13   Mohave game, ca. 1858. Drawing by Balduin Mollhausen. Courtesy of The
     Bancroft Library.

59 Chemehuevi granaries, date and photographer unknown. Courtesy of California Department of Parks and Recreation.

59 Cahuilla granary. From the Frederick Starr Collection 1894-1910, Museum of the American Indian, Heye Foundation. Negative #15495.

59 Pomo granary in Ukiah village, 1922. Photographer unknown. Courtesy of Sun House Archives Collection, Ukiah.

61 Hupa fishing dam, Humboldt County, 1906. Photo by P.E. Goddard. Courtesy of Phoebe Apperson Hearst Museum of Anthropology. Negative #15-3301.

62 Josie Brown Marks, 1928. Photo by T. T. Waterman. Courtesy of Phoebe Apperson Hearst Museum of Anthropology. Negative #15-11473.

62 Little Ike [Fish Ike] (Karuk) fishing from platform (Amaikiara), probably before 1910. Photo by S.A. Barrett. Courtesy of Phoebe Apperson Hearst Museum of Anthropology. Negative #15-17262.

62 Hupa trout dam, 1923. Photo by [Edward S.] Curtis. Courtesy of Humboldt State University. Negative #944.

63 Merk Oliver, 1988. Photo by Jean Perry.

63 Modoc man fishing from boat, 1907. Courtesy Milwaukee Public Museum.

65 Hupa deer hunter with decoy mask, date and photographer unknown. Courtesy of Field Museum. Negative #9562.

68 Lucy and Kathleen Smith, May 1995, shortly after Lucy was honored by Jesse Peter Museum and Kathleen had given a talk about her. Photo by Beverly R. Ortiz.

70 Jennifer Bates, ca. 1992. Photo by Janet Caron-Owens.

71 Elk antler purse made by George Blake, 1989. Courtesy of The Oakland Museum.

72 Stormy Rojas, 1993. Photo by Dugan Aguilar.

73 Ohlone woman, 1791. Drawing by José Cardero. Courtesy of Smithsonian Institution.

73 Women dancers, D-Q University, 1995. Photo by Sadie Cash Margolin.

75 Vivien Hailstone, California State Library, 1989. Photo by Heather Hafleigh. Courtesy of California Indian Project.

76 Basket hat, date and artist unknown. Courtesy of Phoebe Apperson Hearst Museum of Anthropology. Negative #1-27876.

76 Lidded basket by Elizabeth Hickox, date unknown. Photo by Larry Reynolds. Courtesy of Southwest Museum.

77 Rattlesnake basket, date and artist unknown. Courtesy of Phoebe Apperson Hearst Museum of Anthropology. Negative #1-70524.

77 Feathered basket, date and artist unknown. Photo by David Heald. Courtesy of National Museum of the American Indian.

79 Plank canoe, 1988. Photo by Rick Terry. Courtesy of Santa Barbara Museum of Natural History.

80 Balsa, date and photographer unknown. Courtesy of Phoebe Apperson Hearst Museum of Anthropology. Negative #15-18582.

Index

Bold type indicates photo or illustration.